A Bouquet
of
Inspiration

$\mathcal{A}$
BOUQUET
of
INSPIRATION

ENCOURAGEMENT, FRIENDSHIP, COMPASSION, COMFORT, TRUST, LOVE, HOPE

SHARRON MALINE

XULON PRESS

Xulon Press
555 Winderley Pl, Suite 225
Maitland, FL 32751
407.339.4217
www.xulonpress.com

© 2024 by Sharron Maline

All rights reserved solely by the author. The author guarantees all contents are original and do not infringe upon the legal rights of any other person or work. No part of this book may be reproduced in any form without the permission of the author.

Due to the changing nature of the Internet, if there are any web addresses, links, or URLs included in this manuscript, these may have been altered and may no longer be accessible. The views and opinions shared in this book belong solely to the author and do not necessarily reflect those of the publisher. The publisher therefore disclaims responsibility for the views or opinions expressed within the work.

Unless otherwise indicated, Scripture quotations taken from the Holy Bible, New International Version (NIV). Copyright © 1973, 1978, 1984, 2011 by Biblica, Inc.™. Used by permission. All rights reserved.

Paperback ISBN-13: 979-8-86850-227-9
Ebook ISBN-13: 979-8-86850-228-6

Table of Contents

Acknowledgement ix

God is love, hope, peace, and much more 1

We Should Rely on God's Love 3

God's Love Cannot Be Measured 4

God Is Peace 6

God Is There For One And All 7

God's Might Hand. 8

Lord, You Are Precious To Me. 9

There Is Hope. 10

Lord, God, You Are Great 11

Talk to the Shepherd 12

God Won't Give Up On Us 13

One Moment At a Time 14

Don't Worry 15

Lord, God of One and All. 16

My Sins Were Swept Away. 17

Be Still and Listen. 19

Celebrations and Special Occasions. 20

Year Is Over And Done 21

'Twas Not The End Of The Story 22

Easter Blessings. 23

They Cried, Jesus is Guilty. 24

A BOUQUET OF INSPIRATION

One Friday, Many Years Ago 25
Things About To Change 26
Dogwood Bush 27
Easter In the Springtime 28
Springtime, A Favorite Season 29
Honor Mothers Everywhere 30
Happy Mother's Day, Mom 31
A Mother Is A Wonderful Person 32
Mother's Day 33
Memorial Day 34
Father's Day 35
Super Dad 36
Proud American 37
Celebrate Thanksgiving Everyday 38
Most Wonderful Time of the Year 39
The First Christmas Morn 40
Christmas Is Ever So Near 41
What does Christmas Mean to You? 42
Some 2,000 Years ago 43
I'll Be Home For Christmas 45
Another Birthday I Am Celebrating 46
It Is Your Birthday, My Friend 47
Happy Birthday, Friend 48
Happy Birthday to the Love of My Life 49
Aged to Perfection 50
9-11-2001 Anniversary 51
Graduation Day 53
Class of 1961 54
Wedding Proposal 55

A Bouquet of Inspiration

Celebrate Your Marriage. 56
Wedding Prayer 57
Anniversary Song 58
Anniversary Wishes To You 59
You Became a Grandmother 60
Special People In Our Lives 61
Friendship 63
Dedication to My Husband 64
A Tribute to My Dad. 66
Grandparents Are Special 68
Pastor Appreciation 70
A Brother In Christ 71
A Long Time Friend 72
The Lord Called Friends of Mine. 73
When Someone You Love Passes Away 74
He Was My Brother 75
Remembering a Friend 76
My Mother, A Great Friend 77
Mother-in-law, Wonderful and Precious 78
Emotions and Feelings 80
Lord, I Feel so Alone Today 81
Curve Balls In Life 82
Feeling Sad Or Overwhelmed. 83
Lord, I Am Hurting. 84
Tears Keep Falling. 85
Trials and Tribulations 86
I Forgot To Pray 87
A Bittersweet Day 88
We've Been Blessed. 89

A BOUQUET OF INSPIRATION

Blessings We Receive 90

My Husband, Now An Angel In Heaven So High......... 91

His Days Were Numbered 92

I Awoke With A Start................................. 93

Thinking and Dreaming of the Past 94

There Are Times We Moan and Complain............... 95

Pity Party 96

Day Was Gloomy and Gray 97

This is a Sad Time.................................... 98

Trust and Follow the Lord 99

A Masterpiece Am I 101

A Child of God Am I................................. 102

My Child, I'm Calling You 103

To Your Heavenly Home you Went 104

A Special Job... 105

There Is a Purpose and a Plan for Me.................. 106

Be Thankful 107

The Lord Blessed Me With A Special Task.............. 108

Better Days Are Ahead 109

Praises and Songs In My Heart........................ 110

White Staircase Shining In The Light 111

I May Not Be Able, But I Am Willing 112

Why, God, Why 113

What If Mary Did Believe.............................114

I Am A Mother.......................................115

Dandelions Everywhere 116

Forgive and Pray 117

VIII

Acknowledgement

Many people throughout my life have encouraged me to express my thoughts and feelings through poetry. My mother and father always told me that I could do things in life and that I would succeed. My husband was always by my side and encouraged me through all the things that I chose to do at the time. My family and friends were always there to encourage me.

All the words that I write come from God Almighty. I'm so glad that He gave me the words to write so that people could understand the meaning of all my thoughts. Through these words I pray that people will learn to know and trust God in all things.

I hope and pray that my words are filled with hope and encouragement. Writing this book has been a challenge, but also a blessing to me. May God bless each person who reads this book.

Even though my parents and husband have gone to their eternal home to be with God, I still feel as though I get encouragement from them daily. I have many wonderful people who encourage me and pray for me all the time. Three wonderful prayer warriors and helpers are Patti Pearson, Gaye Anderson, and Kaysi Veatch. They have helped compile my book. Thank you, family and friends.

A BOUQUET OF INSPIRATION

Most of all, I give praise and thanks to God for always being by my side through all the trials and tribulation. I knew I could also go to Him for anything. What a mighty God is He.

GOD IS LOVE, HOPE, PEACE, AND MUCH MORE

Do everything in love: faith, hope, and love; and love is the greatest of these. Heart and soul: love never fails. Love is always patient and kind. A friend always loves. Live, laugh, and love.

Love comes when we feel unworthy, and when we are overwhelmed. When we are weary, feeling insecure, and doubting, we are broken. It comes when we just need a hug.

We do not need to earn our way to God. We only need to open our hearts and see that He is already here with us. He told us "I will never leave you or abandon you." Hebrews 13:5

This is the truth, and all our hearts need to know this today. Love came for us. Love will always come for us, and no matter what, He is not leaving us.

God's presence is a gift we don't deserve. He comes close and stays with us through high and low times in our life. He is faithful, true, and the greatest friend you could even ask for.

Know that God loves you and me, and longs for us to take our place in His loving arms. He loves us even though we fail Him every day.

Thank God each day for being there for you. Sometimes we fail to recognize His presence and go our separate ways.

He will be waiting for you when you decide that you need Him and when you ask Him to always be in your life.

Christ is the living hope, the fulfillment of everything we want in life.

Remember, God is a loving God. He will love you no matter what.

We Should Rely on God's Love

God's love is what we should rely on.
Know that He has the best in store for you and me.
What is in the past is over and done,
But for today, be the best that you can be.
Fall on bended knee to pray.
Ask God for guidance in all that you do.
Please, Lord, show me the way.
Help me with each thing that I must go through.
Thank You for the love You have for me.
I want to share your love with one another,
And let them know that in their life, You want to be.
Your love is sufficient for each sister and brother.

God's Love Cannot Be Measured

God's love for us can never be measured.
What He gives to us in life is to be treasured.
He will be there with us, if we let Him, day by day.
He wants to provide our daily needs, if only to Him we
will pray.
He doesn't always answer our prayers the way that we
want Him to,
But He knows what is best for us in all that we do.
Just trust God, and daily in Him believe.
His love for us will never leave.
We need to share His love with each and everyone.
Praise Him daily, until your life is over and done.
Sometimes, to some, it's hard for our love to them, show.
Remember they are all God's children and ask God for your
love to grow.
God loves each person here on earth.
He has had His arms around them from their birth.
For a reason, God has sent them our way.
Sometimes, for them, all we can do is pray.
To Jesus we truly belong,
We are weak but He is strong.
Jesus loves all of His children, this I know,
Because the bible tells me so.

Thank you, Lord, for the love You give to me.
Help me daily to be a blessing to each person that I see.

God Is Peace

Through troubled times each day
We can trust that God is there in every way.
He is there to love, and protect each and everyone
Until our time on earth is over and done.
When our time is over here on earth
To Heaven, God will take us for joy and mirth.
When the storms around us rage and roar,
We don't always know, for us, what God has in store.
We should fall down on our knees
And ask Him to surround us with His peace.
We know that by having God in our lives every day
And by following Him, we will be doing things His way.
Surround me with Your peace, this I ask.
Please, show me what You desire in each of my task.

God Is There for One and All

God never forces Himself on anyone.
He is with one and all, until everything is over and done.
To follow and believe in Him is all that He does ask.
He will be with us and gives us strength through each task.
Why do so many people, in God, do not believe.
That is really hard for me to conceive.
I try to follow God each and every day,
But sometimes I go astray.
I try ever so hard to stay on the right path and ask God
to lead me.
He knows that I am trying to be the best that I can be.
God wants to hold me in His arms and show me the way.
To Him, all He asks of me: to kneel and pray.
Soon I realize that, God, I truly need.
I need to listen to Him, and His words I need to heed.
God forgives me and gives me another day, I'm so glad.
He holds me close when I am confused or sad.
Thank You, God, for always being there for me.
Help me daily to remember all Your promises ever to be.

God's Mighty Hand

God's mighty hand protects me day by day.
He shows me His love in a special way.
Lord, I want to say thank You for all that You do
And for caring for me through and through.
Sometimes it is hard for me to see
Of all the wonderful things that You have planned for me.
Sometimes the bumps in life I must take.
And the best of it, I must make.
I can handle all the things that I face.
God, with Your mighty hands, You will take me through
each day with Your grace
Again, I say thank You, Lord
For all Your mercy and love to me You have poured.

Lord, You Are Precious to Me

My Lord, You are precious to me.
The love I have for You, I hope people can see.
You are there for me all night and day.
When I need to talk to someone, to You I can pray.
Everything I have comes from You
And You are there to help me in all that I do.
For all things, I give You praise from the bottom of my heart.
Help me daily in all my actions and words to do my part.
To a stranger, from me, they might just need a smile
And for another, encouragement for them, I can give to go
the next mile.
I know these things I can do
Because supporting me, by my side, God it is You.
When I don't have the words to say,
I know You will give them to me in a special way.

There Is Hope

Without God there cannot any hope be.
For the future, is not for anyone to see.
Ask God to be with you day by day
And to help you through each difficult way.
Trust and obey God in all that you do
And each day, He will give to you anew.
Rejoice in the hope of the glory of God
And by our faith, our life will be broad.
Be joyful in hope and faithful in prayer.
Confession of your sin, to God, you should bare.
By faith, through the Spirit, we eagerly wait
And in hope, Heaven will be for us at a future date.
When people, in God, do not believe
How can of hope they receive?
By having hope, eternity with God will ever be
For all who believe, including you and me.

LORD, GOD, YOU ARE GREAT

Lord God, You are ever so great.
Things happen in our lives, that we want to celebrate.
In everything, You are with us through and through.
I want to take a moment now to say thank You.
I want to give You praise
For being with me through all of my days.
I know that, in You, I must trust and abide.
You will never leave me and will always be by my side.
What a privilege it is to know You as my Lord.
I appreciate all the care and love to me You have poured.
Things will not always go the way that I have planned,
But You are in control and have everything in Your hand.
Again, thank You is what I want to say.
In Your precious name, this I pray.

Talk to the Shepherd

When at night you can't sleep
Talk to the Shepherd instead of counting sheep.
He is there to listen to your every need.
Ask Him for guidance and, for you, He will lead.
He wants to hear about, in your life, each and everything.
He wants praises to Him, for you to sing.
There's nothing that He can't see you through.
With open arms and a listening ear, He's always
there for you.
To be able to go to the Shepherd to comfort me, I'm so glad.
He holds me tight in His arms even when I am sad.
If I go down the wrong road
He is there to pick me up and help me carry my load.
I'm so glad, when I can't sleep at night
I can go to the Shepherd and He will make things right.
If I feel alone and lost, I always have the Shepherd I
can go to.
I know that He will always love and care for me and you.
Thank You, Lord, for always being there for me.
Your tenderness, love and kindness will forever be.

God Won't Give Up On Us

Lord, I feel that I have gone astray.
Bring me back to You, this I pray.
My feelings and attitude have not been right
Through some days and into the night.
I sometimes feel of my cries, You do not hear.
And at times I shed many a tear.
I know more time I should pray to You.
I ask You to give me strength and wisdom in all that I do.
Sometimes in our life, trials and trouble will be,
But I know through each, God is with me.
He knows of all my hurt and pain.
Through each thing, more love from Him I will gain.
Some things we make a real fuss.
God will never give up on us.
Days that we are feeling low and sad,
Look up to the heavens, thank God and be ever so glad.
Trust in God for the answers we should know.
He will always show us the right way to go.

One Moment at a Time

Give it all to Jesus, one moment at a time.
Going to Him in all that you do is no crime.
He is a friend to me, ever so dear and near.
For me, He always has a listening ear.
He listens to my every need and praise.
He is with me all of my days.
Jesus is never too busy to listen to me.
I thank Him for being in my life ever be.
To me, He is a wonderful friend.
He never judges me, and He will comfort me to the very end.
I know that whatever is on my mind, He listens to what I say.
He loves me and gives me grace each and every day.
Having Jesus by my side, and being my friend, I'm so glad.
He is the best friend that I have ever had.
My thanks and praises with hands held high, to You
Lord, I send.
Thank You, Lord, for being my special friend.

Don't Worry

Worry is one thing that God does not want us to do.
He provides our need daily for me and you.
In God, always, we are to trust.
He cares for us and will make all things just.
When we feel that worry is taking over, bow your
head and pray.
There is nothing that we cannot handle that God will give to
you or me.
He is there for us through all things ever to be.
Your concerns at the foot of the cross lay
And God will take care of us in a special way.
Tell everyone what God has done for you.
Even times of trouble, He is there for you in all that you do.
Jesus loves you and me, this I know.
Now let our love and kindness to everyone show.
Thank You Lord that we can come to you on bended knee.
To be able to bow our heads and pray to You for all to see.

Lord, God of One and All

Lord, God of one and all,
On bended knee, Your name we will call.
We ask for guidance and protection day by day
And to watch over our loved ones in a special way.
For our freedom, soldiers must fight
So, we will be safe every day and night.
For each one, from us apart,
Let them know we love them with all of our heart.
We thank You Lord God for all that You do
And we pray for our loved ones each day anew.
Thanks, and praises to God we sing
For our soldiers to come home that You will safely bring.
To each and every one and God they are very dear.
Know that our words we say, we want You to hear.
If ever in trouble or danger we seem to be,
God is there for all of us, you and me.
To keep our men and woman safe while they are away,
We must trust and pray to God each and every day.
Bring each soldier home to the one they love.
We know that they were watched over and cared for by
God above.

My Sins Were Swept Away

I had a dream one night.
Seeing it, I awoke with a bit of fright.
I saw a Man with long white beard and hair.
A long white robe He did wear.
With such ease and concern, the ground He did sweep.
He was even getting down in the ruts ever so deep.
Into a pile He swept each and everything.
The whole time He was doing this, praises He did sing.
Everything that He had seen seemed to be bad.
It looked a lot like the things that made people mad.
There were sins there that had been committed, that
He did see.
I wondered what He was seeing in me.
He said in a deep voice, 'My child I love you.
I want to forgive all of your sin that you did do,
But first I must sweep it all away.
I want you to start living for me each and every day.
You need to pray by getting down on bended knee
And ask forgiveness and love from Me.
I want to sweep away all of your sin,
But you have to rely on Me again and again.'
I fell on my knees to the ground
And I told Satan, to him, I did not want to be bound.
Peace and comfort, I soon felt in my heart
Knowing by following God was a good start.

A Bouquet of Inspiration

Following God is not always easy to do.
I know He is always there for me and you.
I arose from my knees and around me I did glance.
The pile of sin was gone, knowing that God was giving me a
second chance.
I saw the Man sweeping on another road
I knew that He wanted to ease another person's load.
Ask God to forgive your each and every sin
Knowing that eternal life with God, you will win.
God will also sweep your sin away
If only you will ask Him everyday
So, if it is closeness of God, in your life you want to be
Then pray and fall on your bended knee.

Be Still and Listen

'My child, My child, be still and listen,' God says to me.
'Through good times and bad, with you I will ever be.'
God says, 'I'm in control, now let Me do things My way.
First, I ask that you kneel, bow your head, and pray.
Of everything you say or do, stop and think.
Material things that you have may be gone in a blink.
Pray for the ones, in Me, who do not believe or know.
Tell them of the love to them I will ever show.
Life is short here on earth.
You have been My child since before your birth.
Someday you will come and share My home with Me.
What a glorious time that will be.
While you still have the time, choose what you know is right.
From you, I will take away your fear and fright.
Listen, think, and choose of all the right things to do, that is
all that I ask.
Know that I will be with you through each and every task.
Forever, I want you by My side.
Trust in Me and the things I want you to do, always abide.
Know that I love you in a very special way.
I will provide all your need's day by day'.

Celebrations and Special Occasions

Throughout the year, we have the opportunity to celebrate holidays and special occasions. We have these days to be able to celebrate with family and friends. What a privilege to be able to celebrate. As we celebrate, let us remember to thank God that we can have these days of celebration. Some of the holidays may be hard to get through as we have sad memories of a loved one. But if we ask, God will get us through these days with His love.

Every season of life has a purpose.

As believers, we have many reasons to celebrate. One to remember is that our sins are forgiven. So, let us rejoice and celebrate.

Don't just be an observer on special occasions. Celebrate and let your heart be filled with joy.

Lord, forgive me for so often forgetting all that I have to celebrate. Teach me to celebrate all You have done for me with joy, purity, and thanksgiving.

Romans 11:36b: Celebration reminds us that every success happens by the grace of God.

Year Is Over and Done

One year is over and done
With a new year that has just begun.
There were times when we were happy or sad,
But God was with us, through it all, I'm so glad.
For everyone, God has a plan for us to do.
We need to listen to God everyday through and through.
Sometimes to listen and do what He asks is very hard.
At all times we need to keep up our guard.
We will have challenges and trials day by day.
We need to remember to bow our heads and pray.
We need to ask Him, for us, to lead and guide
Then, for all things, we need to abide.
Every day, to God, we must say thank You
For being with us in all that we do.
At all times, God will be with us ever so near.
To each and every one, may you be blessed throughout
this year.
Be kind and love one another in every way.
Have a prosperous and a happy year day by day.

'Twas Not the End of the Story

'Twas not the end of the story, when on the cross Jesus died.
He knew of His Father's calling, He must abide.
Jesus took the punishment of pain for you and me
Dying on the cross was the thing that needed to be.
With His death, for our sins He paid.
For three days in the grave, He laid.
He arose on the third day and to Heaven He went.
Jesus had accomplished everything for what He
had been sent
From God, eternal life was given to all as a gift.
Trust, obey, and praise Him daily, we should lift
So long ago, that was our very first Easter Day
Lord lead, guide, and direct us in every way.
As you can see, this is the continuance of Jesus' story
Through all of this, now the angels sing of the glory
For what you did for us, Lord, we say thank You.
We want to give You praises for all that You do.

EASTER BLESSINGS

The true meaning of Easter, do you believe?
Then of that Lord's blessing and mercy you will receive.
Jesus was whipped, beaten, and hung on a cross to die.
For this punishment, He took for me, I have a tear
in each eye.
He did this to pay for our every sin
And for this, victory in Heaven, I will win.
He suffered so much for each and everyone.
He hung on the cross until His life here on earth was
over and done.
He did this because of the love He has for you and me.
Someday, because of this I believe, in Heaven with Him I
will ever be.
Thank you, Lord, for taking for each person the pain.
For those who believe, we have much to gain.
He arose from the grave on the third day
And went to be with His heavenly Father in a special way.
Don't doubt that this is true.
Believe this and accept the Lord through and through.
Easter blessings to you, I pray.
Remember this special time each and every day.
The Lord loves you and me.
Take this opportunity and share of this wonderful love for
all to see.
Remember what Jesus did was very clear.
Easter is a special time of the year.

They Cried, Jesus is Guilty

They cried; Jesus is guilty without a doubt.
Crucify Him, crucify Him, they did shout.
The soldiers nailed Him to a cross and hung Him high.
Jesus was hung there until He did die.
Two men hung there with Him, one on each side.
As they hung there, they bowed their heads and cried.
On that day His mother, Mary, many tears did she shed
As she watched while Jesus hung there and bled.
Jesus cried "Forgive them, Father, for they know not
what they do."
Then He cried "it is finished, God I am coming
home to you."
They took Him off the cross and laid Him in a tomb.
All around, you could see the people filled with gloom.
To close the opening of the tomb, a stone was rolled
into place.
The people thought they never again would see Jesus' face.
He took the punishment of sin for you and me,
As this was all of God's plan to be.
On earth, His life for all of us, He gave.
Three days later, Jesus arose from the grave.
He lives, now everyone did shout.
He truly is Christ the King and Savior without a doubt.

One Friday, Many Years Ago

One Friday, many years ago, was a very sad and dark day.
Our Lord, Jesus, paid for our sins in a terrible way.
He was hung on a cross with nails in His hands and feet.
Soon it would be that time again, in Heaven, His Father He
would meet
Jesus knew His life was over and done here on earth.
This is what God had planned for Him from His birth.
He took the punishment for our each and every sin.
He did this so our salvation we would win.
After He took His last breath on the cross, He was laid in a
grave so low,
On the third day, He would rise and to Heaven He would go.
Sunday, the tomb was opened up and He was not there.
Some of the people cried and stood there to stare.
Jesus had overcome death and was alive as this was
God's plan.
He came to earth to take the punishment for every
woman and man.
That Sunday was a happy and glorious day.
Sometimes our lives seem as dark as that Friday.
But be encouraged, the day of rejoicing has come our way.
Christ arose and lives today, let us celebrate
Thank You Lord, we pray, for Your sacrifice for us, we
appreciate.

THINGS ABOUT TO CHANGE

One beautiful day a long time ago,
Things were going to change, this we knew.
Jesus, everyone did praise.
How things can change in just a few days.
People accused Him of a crime and said He should die.
They nailed Him to a cross and hung Him ever so high.
At times, how cruel people can be.
He took the pain and punishment of sin for you and me.
After it was finished, in a tomb, Jesus they did lay.
He arose from the grave on the third day.
With a sigh and a tear in their eye
Jesus is alive, the people did shout and cry.
Christ's sacrifice is what God desired.
The punishment for our sins is what was required.
We can all have peace because the tomb is empty.
For what Christ did for us, thank God on bended knee.

Dogwood Bush

Once the dogwood bush was a tall and stately tree.
But now, it is a flowering bush for all to see.
A cross, from the tree, was to be made.
Jesus was hung on the cross and for our sins, He paid.
He was innocent, but for us, He needed to die.
On a hill, far away, they hung Him ever so high.
The suffering and pain that He went through,
He did this so eternal life could be for me and you.
Since that time so long ago, the tree has never been that tall.
He hung on that cross waiting for God's final call.
The dogwood bush blooms at Easter for all to see.
The flowers form a perfect cross, in remembrance to be.
Down on bended knee, take time to thank the Lord
For Sacrificing His Son and the love to us He has poured.

Easter In the Springtime

We celebrate Easter in the Spring.
It reminds us of the new life the season does bring.
Jesus went to the cross to pay the price for our sin.
And if we believe in Him, eternal life with Him we will win.
For us, the terrible punishment He took.
For the forgiveness of our sins, to Him we should look.
He laid in the tomb for three days
And then on the third day, to Heaven He did raise.
What a glorious sight to see.
We know when the time is right, with Jesus we will
forever be.
Thank You Lord, for the sacrifice You made in a special way.
Easter, oh what a glorious happy day.

Springtime, A Favorite Season

For many, springtime is their favorite season.
Things are all new and fresh and for a good reason.
During the Fall and Winter, God gave the trees and
flowers a rest
So, in the springtime, come up looking their best.
So, refreshing, each have all the colors, each and every hue.
God created this beauty for me and you.
For all the beauty, He wants us to appreciate
And to give Him praises ever so great.
The flowers, He wants us to stop and enjoy each and
every one.
The lovely fragrance will last every day until they are done.
New life in plants and animals comes each and every spring.
We know, that to us, this God does bring.
Sing praises, to God, for all things each and every day.
Ask God to be with each of us in a special way.
I am so glad that God is always by my side
And I know through all things, of me, He asks, I
should abide.
When I need it most, Lord, I ask that You give me rest
So, I can be anew, refreshed and at my best.
Thank You, God, for all the beauty that surrounds me.
Help me to appreciate everything that I can see.

Honor Mothers Everywhere

Mothers everywhere, we want to honor you.
It appears your job is never through.
From early morn until into the night,
You try to teach your children all things that are right.
You comfort them and hold them ever so close
And you even kiss them on their little nose.
When they stumble or fall, you are there
To show them how much you truly care.
When they have tears in their eyes you wipe them away.
For them, daily you bow your head and pray.
All things that you do, they appreciate.
Thank you for being a mother ever so great.
Mother's Day comes but once a year,
But every day to them you are ever so dear.
Maybe our mother is not with us today.
In our hearts the memory of her will always stay.
Thank God for each and every mother
And help us to show our love to one another.
May God's blessing be with each mother everyday
And for her to know, she I loved in a special way.

Happy
Mother's Day, Mom

From both of us, Mom, Happy Mother's Day
You are very special to us in every way.
You have wisdom, strength and grace
And always a smile upon your face.
You are there for each and everyone.
You pray daily for each daughter and son.
Honor, gratitude, and praise we give to you.
God be with you in all that you do.
We love you from the bottom of our heart
And your love for us will never part.
Thank you for being such a wonderful mother.
Help us to always show our love to one another.
God bless you each and every day.
On bended knee, this we pray.

A Mother Is a Wonderful Person

A mother is a wonderful person ever to be.
She sees to the needs of her children and family.
She shows her love to each and everyone
From early morn until day is over and done.
She kisses our booboos and cradles us with love
And knows God is watching over us from above.
On her face, she almost always has a smile
And for one and all, she goes the extra mile.
She gets on her knees and to God she does pray.
With love for us, she does this day by day.
For our future, she tries to prepare us
And does this without nary a fuss.
For each of us, she is forever and always there.
Day by day she shows us how much she does truly care.
We need to tell God daily, for our mother, thank You.
She is a wonderful woman ever so true.
To you, as a mother, I want to say
Hope you have a very special and Happy Mother's Day.

MOTHER'S DAY

Mother's Day, to some women, is filled with gladness,
To others it might be a day of sadness.
God knows of all the joy and each tear.
He is there for us, every moment of the day, that is clear.
Things happen in our lives that we don't understand,
We have to believe that whatever happens, God had
it planned.
Take the time to praise and rejoice in the Lord each and
every day.
Whatever the situation, He is with us all the way.
Your love you can share with one and all.
Do this until, for you, the day He does call.
In many ways, God has blessed you.
Follow and trust Him in all that you do.
May this day be filled with the joy of the Lord.
Remember all of the blessings and the love to you He
has poured.

Memorial Day

On this and every Memorial Day
We should remember our Veterans in a special way.
For the freedom of our country, they did fight.
They knew in their hearts this was right.
They did not know of the perils they might face.
Yet they marched into battle full of God's grace.
Some never came home to their family and a friend,
As they fought the battle until the end.
To each and every military person you see,
Stop and thank them for serving our country.
Appreciation should be shown to each and every one
Until every day is over and done.
A lot of sacrifices, by each one, have been made.
Honor and tribute to each should be paid.
For all of your service, I'd like to say
Because of you, freedom is ours every single day.
To all the military people and their families, God bless you.
May He watch over and protect you in all that you do.

Father's Day

We need to celebrate Father's Day in a special way.
Our earthly father may be with our heavenly Father
on this day.
Memories of our father are very dear
And in our hearts, we will always hold them near.
We need to thank God on bended knee
For letting our father, ever so special be.
Our father, when God did call
Went through Heaven's gate standing ever so tall.
God needed my father, this I know
But because I loved him so, it was hard to let him go.
I am so proud of the earthly father I had
And being his child I am ever so glad
God will always be my Father forever and ever.
His love for me, as His child, will end never.
God, on each and every Father's Day, I want to celebrate
Your love.
Someday I will be there with You in Heaven above.
Thank You, Father God, for wanting and loving me.
Help me be the person that You want me to be.

SUPER DAD

Happy Father's Day, to the super dad, we'd like to say.
Hope this day, for you, is special in every way.
You play with us and take us places.
It seems like you can always put smiles on our faces.
You teach us right from wrong
And you are with us all day long.
We want to say thank you
For all the wonderful things, for us, you do.
God gave you to us to be our dad.
For this we are truly glad.
We will always love you in a very special way.
We want to say, have a wonderful and Happy Father's Day.

Proud American

An American, I am proud to be.
We get to live in a country that is free.
Men and woman fought hard and long
To keep our country ever so strong.
There have been many ups and downs
That have occurred in cities and towns.
Through God's help and grace
Each thing, easy or hard, we can face
Our flag waves each and every day.
For our freedom, we thank God and pray.
On this Independence Day, let us celebrate
The opportunities and freedom we have are great.
Living in America should fill each of us with pride
The laws of the land we should always abide.
God bless the USA
And keep us safe day by day.

Celebrate Thanksgiving Everyday

Thanksgiving Day, once a year, we celebrate.
Giving God thanks and praise every day, is great.
We don't just receive blessings only one day each year.
God blesses us daily, that is clear.
Can you count the blessings you receive each and
every day?
Do you thank God for each one in a special way?
God provides our every need
And daily, for us, He will always lead.
For each and everything you have, tell God thank You.
Thank Him, also, for everything that you can do.
There are times when troubles we face,
But God blesses us with His grace.
Remember daily, not just once a year, give God thanks
and praise.
Thanksgiving should be celebrated on all the days.
Thank You Lord, I pray on bended knee
For what You provided and the love You give to me.

Most Wonderful Time of the Year

Christmas is the most wonderful time of the year.
It is when we celebrate Jesus Christ's birthday, ever so dear.
As a baby, He came to earth to grow.
As He got older, He would teach people the way to go.
When He was born, the angels began to sing
"Praises to the newborn King."
In the stable with animals all around
Came from the newborn baby: a wonderful sound.
The shepherds and wise men came from afar.
They would find the new King by following the bright star.
It was such a wonderful night
To be able to see the beautiful sight.
From the beginning, He knew what His life would be.
He was sent to take the punishment for you and me.
He would have many trials to go through
But He knew it was something God had sent Him to do.
Be ever so grateful of that wonderful event.
Know of the reason that He was sent
Fall on your knees and pray
And thank God for sending His Son on that special day.
Jesus will be with you through and through
To watch over and care each day for you.
Merry Christmas to you I'd like to say
May you be blessed each and every day

THE FIRST
CHRISTMAS MORN

'Twas the night before the first Christmas morn.
When Jesus Christ was to be born.
The people had gathered in Bethlehem for the census count.
They were there when the angels would sing from
the mount.
Of this wonderful event, the people did not understand.
Jesus Christ would be the King and Savior over all the land.
Jesus came as a babe, in a stable His head would lay
God sent His Son and He would take the punishment of our
sin one day.
Then angels sang of the wonderful news on that night.
The stars in the skies shone very bright.
The shepherds left their flock and to the manger they came.
They wanted to see the babe and Jesus Christ was His name.
Remember Jesus is the reason to celebrate Christmas Day.
Blessings to you and your family this Christmas
season, I pray.

Christmas Is Ever So Near

Christmas time is ever so near.
This is my favorite time of the year.
God gave the perfect gift to us on that first Christmas Day.
He sent His Son to earth in a very special way.
The animals in the stable were there to celebrate
Of Jesus Christ's birth that would be great.
The animals said to each other.
Let us celebrate and share the joy with one another.
The sky became very bright
With all of the stars shining so bright.
The angels sang with gladness and joy
For the birth of Jesus, the Baby Boy.
The wise men came to see the newborn King
Everyone sang, to God, Hallelujah, and glad tidings You
did bring.
For this perfect Christmas gift, that God gave to one and all.
Thank God daily and upon your knees fall.
Merry Christmas to each and everyone
Share this wonderful news with all until day is
over and done.

What does Christmas Mean to You?

What does Christmas mean to you?
Do you show the true meaning in all that you say and do?
The perfect gift, we should give to everyone
Is to show the love of God until our time on earth is
over and done.
Expensive gifts do not have to be
Just share God's love for all to see.
A nice compliment or even a smile
Can be given to anyone along each mile.
Help those who are in need
And ask God, for them, to lead.
God gave us the perfect gift.
Praises for this, to God we should lift.
God sent His Son to earth to save each of us.
His wonderful name is Jesus.
Salvation, He wants to give to one and all.
So, we can spend eternity with Him when He does call.
This is the meaning of Christmas ever so true.
Share the spirit of Christmas all year through.
Thank You Lord, for this wonderful gift You have
given to me.
Your love for me will always with me be.

Some 2,000 Years ago

Some 2,000 years ago, on a clear night
A star in the East shone very bright.
It shone over where born was a King.
The angels rejoiced as they did sing.
The shepherds and the wise mean went to see
Of the exciting news that came to be.
Jesus was the baby's name.
To earth, to save us from our sin, He came.
People from very far and near were excited about His birth.
They shouted with Joy that Jesus Christ has been
born on earth.
That was the very first Christmas day.
Today, we celebrate the birth of Jesus in a very special way.
To us, each and every one, God gave us the greatest gift.
His Son was given to us in love and for this our praises we
should lift.
That gift that You, God gave to each and everyone.
We will thank You daily until our lives are over and done.
Help us to remember why, Christmas we celebrate.
Your love for everyone is truly great.
We want to praise You for all You did and continue to do.
Your love for us continues through and through.
We thank You for sending Your Son to us in a special way.
Help us always to remember the reason we celebrate
Christmas Day.

A BOUQUET OF INSPIRATION

Today in the city of David, a Savior has been born, He is
Christ the Lord. Luke 2:11

I'll Be Home for Christmas

I'll be home for Christmas, my true love said to me.
He went to his heavenly home, to be with Jesus for eternity.
The memories of him I hold very dear.
He will always be in my heart, ever so near.
This is a time of sadness and joy.
I know of his life here on earth, he did enjoy.
I am so thankful that in my life, for me he was there.
I know for me, my family and friends, he truly did care
He will, forever, be missed by one and all.
I know that to his heavenly home he went, when
Jesus did call.
The memories of our life together will always be
in my heart
Even though my loved one, from me, did depart.
I know someday, again, my loved one I will see.
And together, with God, we will spend eternity.
God, thank You for my loved one, to me, You did send.
For this, my gratitude to You will never end.
I'll be home for Christmas, my loved one said, and he
was right.
He is now celebrating his homecoming with God every day
and night.

ANOTHER BIRTHDAY I AM CELEBRATING

Another birthday I'm celebrating today,
For this, I thank You, God, and pray.
Each day You awaken me
To be the best that I can be.
How many more birthdays I will have, I do not know.
I do know that You will always be with me though.
My job is not finished yet, here on earth.
You have had my days numbered even before my birth.
Each day You are there, for me, to lead and guide.
When You ask me to do something, I need to abide.
Many more birthdays I want to celebrate,
So, I can let people know that You are ever so great.
For my wonderful life You have given to me,
Praises and thanks I give to Thee.
Show me the way to go each and every day
On bended knee, to You I pray.
For the many blessings through the years on me, You
have poured
For another birthday I am privileged to have,
thank You Lord.

It Is Your Birthday, My Friend

It is your birthday, my friend.
Birthday wishes and blessings to you I send.
A milestone in life you did achieve.
On this day, warm wishes from family and friends you
will receive.
Another year you get to celebrate.
For that, I think that is great.
Throughout your life, you have been blessed each and
every day.
God has poured His love upon you in a special way.
It is your day, enjoy it and have some fun.
Celebrate until the day is over and done.
Ahead for you, many birthdays are in store.
To you I say, Happy Birthday and many more.

Happy Birthday, Friend

It's your birthday and I want to say
Hope your day is special in every way.
You are a good friend ever so dear.
For everyone, you have hugs, smiles, and a listening ear.
Our friendship, I truly treasure.
Of all the good things that you do, I can't even measure.
Your family and friends, I know you truly do care
And your love for each one, you truly share.
This is a day for you to celebrate.
Having a birthday is ever so great.
May our friendship last forever
Through each trail and endeavor.
Happy birthday and God bless you day by day
And for you, I will always pray.

Happy Birthday to the Love of My Life

I have looked high and low for a different way to say
To the love of my life, Happy Birthday.
I can tell you from the bottom of my heart
That I have loved you from the very start.
In every way, you are there for me
And your love for me is the greatest ever to be.
It appears you are always by my side
And for us, God did always lead and guide.
We may not always agree on everything.
But to you, birthday wishes I bring.
Thank you for being my husband and friend.
Just know that for you, my love will never end.
Happy birthday and good wishes for many more birth-
days for you.
Enjoy your birthday all day through.

Aged to Perfection

It's your 80th birthday, hooray, hooray.
Birthday wishes, I am sending your way.
A milestone in life you did achieve.
For this day, warm wishes from family and friends, you
will receive.
You have received many blessings from the Lord.
Each day, from Him to you, His love He has poured.
A birthday is a time to celebrate.
For all of the birthdays you had, that is great.
Happy birthday to you, I say.
You are a special person in every way.
Many more birthdays, I pray for you.
Have fun and enjoy the day in all that you do.

9-11-2001 ANNIVERSARY

9-11-2001, for the USA, was a very tragic day.
Forever, we will remember it in every way.
This couldn't happen in our country, or so we thought,
Because of the many years, for freedom, that was dili-
gently fought.
How could this have happened; we have all asked why.
We don't understand why so many people, on that day,
had to die.
We know God is in control of everything.
Soon God, for us, peace He will bring.
It has been some years since that tragic date.
For each of us, we do not know of our own fate.
Keep faith and trust in the Lord.
Know of all of His love, to us, He has poured.
Pray and praise God each and every day.
Remember to please Him in all the things that we
do and say.
Let us ask God that another 9-11 never happens again.
Tragedies and pain will continue to happen until the world
is free from sin.
For all things that go on in our country, we need to be aware.
And show the people around us, that for them, we care.
Remember all of the families and our country on this anni-
versary day.

A Bouquet of Inspiration

Honor, and respect, God, our country, and our flag in
every way.
Thank You Lord for this and every day.
We ask that You will be with us in a special way.

Graduation Day

For you, it is your graduation day.
Congratulations is what I'd like to say,
This is quite an accomplishment for you.
As your life continues, may God always see you through.
There will be many challenges in your life,
Just learn to take everything in strife.
For you, God has a plan.
He just asks of you to do the best that you can.
Daily, ask God to lead and guide.
Listen to Him and always abide.
Trust and obey Him in all that you do
And He will always be there for you.
May God bless you each and every day,
And to watch over and protect you, is what I pray.

Class of 1961

We graduated in the year 1961.
On that day we shouted hooray, our high school days are
over and done.
We each went our separate way.
We weren't sure what things, in the future, would happen
day by day.
Of some things, we don't understand.
Our life didn't always go as we had planned.
Throughout our life, many challenges we would face.
We got through each one with God's grace.
We didn't know of our friends, if again we would ever see.
But the memories we have of them will forever be.
There were some days that were filled with tears
and sadness.
We also have many days filled with joy and gladness.
Many years later, we came together to celebrate.
Through the years to us, God has been ever so great.
Enjoy all things each and every day under the sun.
Best wishes and blessings to the Alumni of the class of 1961.

Wedding Proposal

One day you asked the love of your life
If she would become your forever wife.
She said yes instead of nay.
Congratulations to you both, I'm sending your way.
Through your married life together, there may be
some frowns.
But with God's grace, you will have more ups than downs
Most of your days will be filled with many a smile.
Know that God will be with you through each and
every mile.
Trust and follow the Lord each and every day.
Never forget, for all things, to Him pray.
May your love for each other be ever so strong.
I pray that your life together will be very long.
Always love one another each and every day through
and through
Remember to finish the day by telling each other I love you.
Pray with each other day by day.
I ask God to bless you in a special way.

Celebrate Your Marriage

Today, your marriage we want to celebrate.
Your love for each other is truly great.
You are a perfect couple; this God did know.
Now to family and friends, your love you can show.
Trust and love each other, in your marriage do.
Be kind and respect your spouse every day through
and through.
Your life together, may it be long.
Side by side through each endeavor, you will be strong.
Through your married life, you have your ups and downs.
You will cry, laugh, smile, and even have a few frowns.
God will be with you through each and every task.
Guidance and strength, He will give, if you only ask.
Praises be to the Lord throughout your married life
As you walk down the path as husband and wife.

WEDDING PRAYER

On this, your wedding day
When the two of you say I do.
Trust in God and follow His way
And He will always watch over you.
Make God the head of your household.
Pray to Him on a daily basis.
His love for you has been told
Throughout the Bible in many places.
Take your loved one by the hand.
Leave your parents and become one.
Walk side by side through the times of sand.
Thank God daily for your loved one when day is done.
Continue to love and share with your mate
All of your love, problems, and gladness.
Promise to your mate never to hate
Even though some days may be filled with sadness.
Remember how much in love you are on this day.
Never let anyone or anything come between the two of you.
Hold on to each other in every way
Through love and kindness, this is the thing to do
Let the love of God shine through
All of your actions, words, and deeds in all places.
Show people what your marriage means to you
Through your shining, smiling faces.

Anniversary Song

One day, many years ago,
I met a man who became my beau.
We knew we were really in love
When we heard bells ringing from above.
We decided to marry and unite as one
And to remain this way until our days were over and done.
We didn't know if our days together were many or few.
We walked down the aisle and told each other I do.
We have, over the years, had good and bad days.
Sometimes, we even wanted to go our separate ways.
We prayed to God day by day.
We knew He would always show us the way.
We knew we were always to love our mate.
We were told by the Lord above, never to hate.
Our children, the best we could, we'd raise.
Every day to God, we would give Him praise.
We are happier now than the day we met.
We knew of our problems, that we should never fret.
The Lord told us follow Him day by day
And I will be with you every step of the way.
Our anniversary, we are celebrating today.
Our desire is for many more anniversaries, this we pray.
Let us honor and cherish each other every day through
and through.
May we always be able, to one another, to say I love you.

Anniversary Wishes To You

The day you got married was a special day for you.
On that day, you said to each other, I do.
An anniversary you are going to celebrate.
Your love for each other is really great.
Over the years, you have had your ups and downs.
You have had many more joyous times than frowns.
You should be proud of the things you have done.
You have been there for each other every day under the sun.
You have been blessed with a beautiful and won-
derful family.
Thank God, for all things, each and every day on
bended knee.
God had been with you through and through.
At all times, God has watched over and protected you.
The love and respect, for each other you show every day.
Many more years together, for you I pray.
May your love for one another never end.
Congratulations and blessings to you I send.

You Became a Grandmother

A Grandmother you have become, congratulations to
you I say.
I know of this day, to the Lord you did pray.
He sent a baby girl as a granddaughter for you.
To love and enjoy every day through and through.
Let each day be filled with fun and joy.
Watch her play with each doll and toy.
A child from God is a gift.
For this child, your praises, to Him, you should lift.
With her, as she grows, show her much love.
Tell her that God sent her as your granddaughter
from above.
This is truly a blessing from the Lord.
On your family, much love He has poured.
For this wonderful baby girl, God has sent your way.
Thank God for this wonderful gift day by day.

Special People in Our Lives

The human soul is a lonely thing; it must have the assurances of companionship. Left entirely to itself, it cannot enjoy anything. God said in the beginning, it is not good that man should dwell alone. Genesis 2:18 People are a body not intended to function separately. God's children are guaranteed the richest and truest friendship both here and hereafter. Only in a true friendship and true love do we find a genuine basis for peace. The only cohesive power in the world is Christ. He alone can bind hearts together in genuine love.

Friendship is truly one of the greatest gifts in life. In our friends, we find trusted companions who know and love us for who we are, no matter what. Our friends are the people who get us through rough times. They always have the right words for us. When we find ourselves taking these important relationships for granted, we should look to the good book for a little reminder about how important friends are.

We all have one friend in common and He is ever so close. His name is Jesus. Aren't you glad that we can rely on Him to be our friend? He is always there for us night and day. Proverbs 18:24 One who has unreliable friends soon come to ruin, but there is a friend that sticks closer than a brother.

John 13:35

A Bouquet of Inspiration

By this all men know ye are my disciples, if ye have love for one another.

Galatians 6:2

Carry each other's burdens and in this way you will fulfill the law of Christ.

Friendship

Through life, friendship is one of the sweetest joys around.
Having friends is a treasure that is truly found.
Friendship is something you don't want to take for
granted ever.
It would be very sad, if a friend, you had never.
Whenever we feel alone, know that there is a friend nearby.
Call on them and then your feelings will feel ever so high.
A friend will love and care for us just the way we are,
Whether they be from you, near or far.
Remember, the only way to have a friend is to be one.
Let your smile and love shine through until all is
said and done.
Cherish your friends, one and all
As they are there for you when down you fall.
Friendship is the greatest gift ever to be had.
Friends walk beside you through good times and bad.
The Lord puts special friends in our life each and every day.
Thank Him daily for sending a friend your way.

Dedication to My Husband

To my loving husband, ever so dear.
You went to your heavenly home and can't, with me, be here.
Some time ago, you left earth to go to Heaven forever be.
You are now with God spending eternity.
I still miss you so.
There are times that I think I feel your presence though.
Together, we had many good years.
We shared good times and even some tears.
For each other, we were always there,
Showing each other how much we did care.
Remembering all the good times is truly a pleasure
And of these memories, I will forever treasure
I wish you were still by my side,
But when God called you, you did abide,
Many children, some not our own, we did raise
And we taught them all, to God, always give praise.
For all of the days, together we had
I'm ever so glad.
A couple, we were always meant to be.
God chose us, me for you and you for me.
If I had to do it all over again, I would marry you.
I was so proud on our wedding day when we each said I do.
I thank God daily for our life we did share.

A Bouquet of Inspiration

For each other we prayed and did care.
My love, for you, will go on forever and a day
Then someday again, we will be together in a special way.
Thank you for choosing me for your wife ever to be.
Our love for each other was always there for all to see.

A Tribute to My Dad

I pay a special tribute to you, Dad, on this Father's Day.
For you, every day, I pray.
You have always been there for me,
Through ups and downs, you taught me to go to God on
bended knee.
You taught me right from wrong
And for this I thank you all my life long.
Together, many special times we have had.
Because you being my dad, I am ever so glad.
I have always been able to come to you regardless
of my need.
I thank God that you are my dad, and for me, the right way
you did lead.
I could not have asked for a better dad than you.
You have and show the love of God, through every-
thing you do.
Things happen in our lives, and we don't know why.
I know if we put our trust in God, He will be there even
when we cry.
God will be there for us each and every day.
He wants us to ask Him daily, for our needs in our lives
when we pray.
Thank you for being such a good example to me.
I pray that I can share your love, you taught me, for
all to see.

A Bouquet of Inspiration

You're a very special dad in all that you do.
I want you to know how much I really love you.

Grandparents Are Special

When I was told that a grandparent I would soon be
I was filled with excitement and glee.
I knew that being a grandparent would be very
special to me
Of the many smiles, kisses, and hugs there would be.
From God, all grandparents are a very special gift
And every day, our praise to Him we should lift.
We give of our love and concern for our grandchildren, each
and everyone.
As grandparents, we will give of our love until time is done.
To each child, there are many things that we can teach
Because our knowledge goes as far as we can reach.
It is an honor for all grandparents on this special day
To be thanked with the love by our grandchildren in
every way.
A child knows that a grandparent is special and full of love
And all of the children are taught of God's love from above.
Sometimes the grandchildren the grandparents will raise
Holding and loving them all of their days.
Grandparents are very special indeed
Knowing of ways, for their grandchildren they will lead.
Thank God for each and every grandparent on this earth

A Bouquet of Inspiration

Knowing that they loved their grandchildren from
their birth.
Grandparents, to the fullest live each day
And for your grandchildren, daily you should pray

Pastor Appreciation

Pastor, with great appreciation, I'd like to say
Thank you for preaching the Lord's word in a special way.
The love of God, shows through and through
In all that you say and do.
You are there for one and all, if they ask.
With a smile on your face, you are ready for every task.
On bended knee, daily, to God you pray.
You ask Him to lead and guide you in a special way.
I am thankful you are my pastor and friend.
I know you will show the love to everyone until the very end.
For you and your family, I ask God to bless you
In all the things that you say and do.
Live your life to the fullest each and every day
For wisdom and strength from God, for you, I pray.

A Brother In Christ

I knew a man who was a brother in Christ and a
friend indeed.
He always had a hug and kind words for those in need.
When my mood was low and down,
He would make me smile instead of frown.
Sometimes a piece of chocolate he would give to me.
He said it would make my troubles flee.
A chuckle from me soon came around.
Then I would thank the Lord for the friend that I had found.
He trusted and loved the Lord every day.
He knew whatever happened to him was God's way.
Our life may be long or short here on earth
God had our days numbered from our birth.
My friend was a prayer warrior each and every day.
He said for me, he would pray.
God opened up His arms one day and told my friend,
'Come home to me.'
He would now be free of pain, and with God, he would
spend eternity.
Indeed, he was a true friend to me.
Now he is with the Lord sitting by His knee.
Someday again, we will meet
When we gather at the Lord's feet.
Lord, thank You and to You I pray.
For sending that person as my prayer warrior and
friend my way.

A Long Time Friend

A longtime friend who was very dear to me,
From earth she passed, and to Heaven, went to be.
Many things, together, we did do.
We would visit with each other and travel too.
The things we did together were great enjoyment and fun.
Sometimes, it would be from early morn until day was done.
A lot of places we did visit and sights to see.
She was always ready to go on adventures with me.
We would put on our tennis shoes and boogie
down the road.
Good times we would have until it was time to return to
our abode,
Many things we would talk about and share.
For each other, we truly did care.
There were times we would laugh and other times we
would cry.
When it was time to leave each other, we would hug and
say goodbye.
She's at peace now with the Lord forever and a day
Sometime again, we will be together, this I pray.
She will be missed by friends and family.
For the time we got to share, I give thanks to God daily.
To me, she was a very dear and wonderful friend.
I am so glad for her in my life, that God did send.

The Lord Called Friends of Mine

Friends of mine, the Lord did call.
They went to be with Him, walking ever so tall.
When the Lord called them by name, they did abide.
Now they are walking with the Lord, by His side.
For them, no more suffering or pain
They knew that eternity with the Lord, they would gain.
The memories of my friends I will forever treasure.
Their friendship to me was dear and a pleasure.
In their lives, there were good times and bad.
And when they had to leave us, it made us sad.
Face to face, again we will meet
And they will be waiting at Heaven's gate, for us, to greet.
Thank You Lord for the friendship I got to share.
I know for their family and friends they did care.
Lord, I want to share my friendship with one and all
And to be of help to them when they call.
Lord, lead, guide, and direct me in every way.
Help me to be a good friend, I pray.

When Someone You Love Passes Away

When someone you love passes away
It is sometimes hard to get through each day.
God will help you in all that you do.
Each step you take, He is always with you.
There are so many firsts you must face.
Each one you can get through with God's grace.
You wonder how you will get through.
Pray to God and He will show you what to do.
Each event is good to remember everyone.
Tears you may shed until the day is over and done.
Remember the good times that you and loved ones
got to share.
Sometimes we feel that life is not fair.
God's plan, we don't always understand.
Through these times, God will hold your hand.
He will lead and guide you through each task.
If only to God, you will pray and ask.
In your heart, the memories will always be clear.
Hold on to those memories, that to you, are ever so dear.

HE WAS MY BROTHER

My brother, a very special person, was he.
His love and care were there for all to see.
A stranger, he never met.
He never had a worry or a fret.
A smile was always on his face.
When you saw him, you knew he was blessed with
God's grace.
He was different from others around in a special way.
His life was filled with joy and love day by day.
When God, to him, He did call
My brother went through Heaven's gate walking tall.
God said, 'come child and be with Me
Together we will spend eternity'.
Someday, with open arms, we will meet.
And with his love and hugs, me he will greet.
I'm so glad for the special moments we had
And having him as my brother, I'm ever so glad.
I thank God day by day
For being able to have my brother in a very special way.

Remembering a Friend

I'd like to take a moment to remember a friend today.
She was special in every way.
She loved her family and Jesus with all her heart.
It was time, from earth, for her to depart.
Her name, Jesus did call.
She walked toward Him ever so tall.
In my life, I'm glad I could call her friend.
I know, for her, Jesus did send.
She will be missed here on earth.
The Lord had her days numbered before her birth.
With a tear in my eye
To her I said goodbye.
Someday, again we will meet.
With a smile and a hug for each of us, we will greet.
For my friend You sent to me, Lord,
I want to say thank You, for on her Your love You poured.

My Mother, A Great Friend

My mother was a great friend to me.
She cared for me with love and kindness for all to see.
My mother went to be with the Lord some time ago.
I loved her so much and I miss her so.
Her job, as a mother, here on earth, had to end
And I thank God for her, to me, He did send.
Her memory will always be in my heart,
Even though for a short time we had to part.
There are things for her, I wished I had done.
Telling her more of the love I had for her is one.
I thank God for the wonderful mother I had
And every day that I had her in my life, I am ever so glad.
She taught how to love one another
And now I am a mother.
Help me, dear Lord, to be the mother that You
want me to be.
Let Your light, each and every day, shine through me.
Blessings for each of my family members, I ask of You,
Dear Lord, each day through and through.

Mother-in-law, Wonderful and Precious

My mother-in-law was wonderful and precious to me.
Her kindness and love, in my heart, will always be.
I was so happy to marry her son.
She told us 'Blessings to both of you until your life is over
and done'.
She was a good part of my life for many years.
Now saying goodbye to her, I shed many tears.
I know for family, daily, she did pray,
Asking God to lead and guide them in a special way.
Throughout her life, she was a good example to all.
Now, to her, God did call.
He said to her, 'on earth you have finished your task
And now come home to Me, is what I ask'.
In her life, she had ups and downs,
But through time, she had more smiles than frowns.
She was always there for you in your time of need
And in prayer, with you, she would lead.
She has blessed many people far and near.
The love she had for everyone was very clear.
At peace, she is now in Heaven with friends and family.
And with God, our heavenly Father, she will spend eternity.
God now holds her close by His side.

As a loving and caring woman, when God called her, she
did abide.
She was to me, a wonderful mother-in-law and friend.
Thanks, and love, to her in Heaven, I want to send.

Emotions and Feelings

Your heavenly Father longs for your life to be marked by emotional joy, fulfillment, satisfaction, and peace. He longs for your emotions to be rooted and grounded in His steadfast love and goodness. Our God is an emotional God. He is not void of feelings.

We feel because He feels. We have emotions because we are made in His image. We are robbed of having our emotions rooted in God whenever we take on more pressure than we are meant to carry. Our emotional health is directly linked to our level of trust. We all have emotions, and we always will; they are part of being human.

Emotional stability should be one of the main goals of every believer. We should seek God to learn how to manage our emotions and stop them.

Peace, I leave with you; my peace I give to you. Not as the world gives do I give to you. Let not your hearts be troubled, neither let them be afraid. John 14:27

For our heart is glad in Him because we trust in His Holy name. Psalms 33:21

Lord, I Feel so Alone Today

Lord, I feel so alone and lonely today.
There are people around me, who say for me they will pray.
I know, Lord, I should rely more on You
I know that You are with me in all that I do.
Sometimes guilty I feel, when no I say to people when
they ask of me
Of things they want me to do and things to oversee.
I can be busy in life with many a task.
Sometimes I feel like I'm hiding my feelings behind a mask.
My true feelings I keep from people, so they won't know
Of how much I'm hurting inside and feeling so low.
I know I need to praise You, God, each and every day.
Even though I feel that things are not going my way.
Everyday blessings from God fall on me.
It might be a beautiful sunrise or a sunset to see.
Lord, calm my spirit and let me know You more.
Please walk with me through every door.
I know, Lord, that for me, You truly do love and care.
With others Your love, I need to share.
Thank You Lord for all that You do for me
Help me to do the best in life that I can be.

Curve Balls in Life

In life, we are thrown curve balls every day.
Sometimes, we don't know where to go, then to God we pray.
Trust the Lord and be strong.
He will be there, always, for us all day long.
Why so many troubles do I have, I ask.
In everything I do, I know the Lord is with me through
every task.
There are days, strong I just cannot be.
Then I remember that Jesus truly loves me.
He will not leave me, even if sometimes I make the
wrong choice.
For a moment, I lost the sound of His voice.
Then to reality, back I came with my eyes opened wide,
I know that Jesus will always be by my side.
If things get too tough for me,
He will pick me up and carry me ever to be.
Thank You, Lord, for opening up my eyes
And helping me see the world full of lies.
I know that I will feel alone some days,
But I still need to take time and give You praise.
Thank You, Lord for holding me close to You.
Please be with me in all that I do.

Feeling Sad or Overwhelmed

Sadness or overwhelmed we may feel at any one time.
But looking for joy and pleasant things is no crime.
Maybe a compliment has just been given to you.
Thank that person and smile as you do.
You can find joy when you make someone smile.
This can change your attitude for awhile.
The beauty around you can be enjoyed every day.
Thank the Lord for these things and your good mood
will stay.
Sometimes we need to rest and be still.
We need to listen to the Lord as we climb each hill.
He will also be with us when we feel we are in a valley
ever so deep.
This is a promise that He will always keep.
Ask God to send you joy each and every day.
Remember to fall on your knees daily and to the Lord, pray.

Lord, I Am Hurting

Oh Lord, I am hurting so much today.
It appears everything is going the wrong way.
So overwhelmed am I
All I can do is cry.
I know You are always with me
And You know what is going to be.
Help me to understand
And, please Lord, hold my hand.
I know Your love for me is ever so great.
And for this I truly appreciate.
Help me to accept what is before me
And open my eyes, so that the outcome, I can see.
Lord I want to trust and obey You,
But sometimes, I feel it is hard to do.
I want to follow Your lead.
Thank You Lord for providing my every need.

Tears Keep Falling

Down my cheeks the tears keep falling, why, oh why?
It seems like, dear Lord, they go from morning until nigh.
Sometimes it is really hard to find joy on certain days.
Yet I know, through all things, I need to give God praise.
He knows the suffering and pain I am going through
And He wants me to know His love for me is ever so true.
Step by step, God is with me day by day.
I just need to listen, and in Him, trust and obey.
Hold me close, dear Lord, this I ask of You.
Give me wisdom and strength in all that I do.
Glory to You, God on high, I want to give.
For a wonderful life, I want to live.
Dry my tears one by one
And soon I will have joy until all is over and done.
Help me to be the person that You want me to be
And let Your love, every day, shine through me.
I am Your child, please bless me day by day.
Thank You for everything, Lord, this I pray.

Trials and Tribulations

We all have trials and tribulations that we go through.
Every day we have, it will be fresh and new.
Let the love of God show upon my face.
We will know that we have been blessed by God's grace.
Through our lives, mistakes we will make.
If we ask, God will show us which path to take.
Without God, how can a person live his life right?
Fall on bended knee to thank God every day and night.
I'm so glad that God is watching over me
His love for me will forever be.
Your child, God, I am this I know.
God take my hand and lead me everywhere I go.
God, for me, has a reason.
He wants me to be productive in every season.
A difference in people's lives I can make, this I know.
Through God's guidance, the way for me to go, He will show.
For everything that takes place in my life, God, thank You.
Lead, and guide me every day through and through.

I Forgot to Pray

Lord, I wondered why things weren't going right today.
Maybe it's because I forgot to pray.
Things went from bad to worse.
I just wanted to curse.
I stopped in my tracks and knelt down.
I knew that God had on His face a frown.
I forgot to take time to give Him praise.
For being there for me all the days.
It only takes a moment or two
To take the time to thank Him for all that He does do.
Don't forget to take the time
In silence to pray to God, is not a crime.
Things will get better, you will see,
If you stop and ask God, in your life ever to be.
Lord, forgive me for not taking time to pray
And be with me each and every day.

A Bittersweet Day

Today was bittersweet for me.
It would have been my anniversary, you see.
Together, we spent many wonderful years
My husband went to Heaven some time ago and I was filled
with tears.
The Lord was good and generous to us each day.
Through our marriage, God was with us in every way.
Many good memories of our life together, I will
always treasure.
Being married to my husband was a great pleasure.
We had our ups and downs,
And many smiles and a few frowns.
The Lord blessed us with a wonderful family
And for this, thankful I will always be.
It is a struggle, without him, some of the time
And missing him is not a crime.
Someday, in Heaven, again we will meet
A day of our reunion will be so neat.
I know, I can go on with God's grace each and every day.
As He will be with me all the way.
Lord, for my wonderful husband I had, thank You.
I ask that You continue to bless me through and through.

We've Been Blessed

Being married, God has blessed us with another year.
Most of the time has been great, but occasionally, we
shed a tear.
We were there for each other every day.
We prayed to God that He would always, in life, show
us the way.
I've said it many times before
And I will continue to say, 'each day I love more and more'.
Sometimes it seems like we were just wed yesterday.
We are now celebrating another anniversary day.
You are my husband and I am ever so proud.
I want to shout from the mountain top, my love for you,
ever so loud.
I want you to know how much for you I care,
And all the time, for each other, we are there.
I know if I had to do it all over again, I would marry you.
I am pretty sure that you would also say I do.
Together, we go through many things each and every day.
We are there for one another in a very special way.
I don't tell you often enough thank you.
I truly appreciate, for me, the many things you do.
Happy anniversary to my husband ever so dear.
I pray that together, we can be for many a year.

Blessings We Receive

Things that we have are blessings, from God, that we receive
Of this I truly believe.
There are things we take for granted every day.
For everything, we should always thank God when we pray.
When you feel down and blue about anything
Take the time and, to God, praises you should sing.
Count your blessings one by one
And you will be happier when the day is over and done.
Even for the little things that happen day by day
Be thankful for them in every way.
Your life will be better when thanks to God you give.
It will make you stronger each day that you live.
Everything you have in life you can be thankful for.
Know, that to you, God's love, He will pour.
Remember that God is with you through each and
everything.
Praises to Him, daily, you should sing.
Be counting your blessings, soon, on your face will
be a smile.
God will be with you each and every mile.
Thanksgiving does not happen only one day of the year.
Giving thanks everyday makes God ever so near.

My Husband, Now an Angel In Heaven So High

To my husband, now an angel in Heaven so high.
When I think of you, I get a tear in each eye.
Today, we would have celebrated your birthday, if you
were here.
You're not, but in my heart, you are very near.
A lot of days, together we did spend,
Each and every one was ever so great, until the end.
God planned for us, a couple to be.
Now you are with God spending eternity.
Each and every day I miss you.
I ask God daily, without you, to get me through.
Someday, when the time is right, we will again meet.
That day will be so neat.
Until that time, I ask God to lead and guide me.
I want to be the best, for everyone, that I can be.
The love that together we shared,
I know that for me you truly cared.
To my husband, if you were here, Happy Birthday is what
I'd like to say.
I know you are always with me in a special way.

His Days Were Numbered

It has been some time since my husband passed away from
this earth.
God, You had his days numbered from his birth.
I thank You for the time, with him, I got to spend.
My love for him will never end.
He was beside and with me in so many ways
Without my husband, hard are some of the days.
Together, a wonderful life we had
And when he left me, I was very sad.
I sometimes think that he is still here
And there are days I think I feel his presence ever so near.
He was such a wonderful, loving husband to me
And our love for each other, we wanted everyone to see.
We had plans of things we were going to do.
Before we got to do them, God, he went to be with You.
Help me Lord through all things, this I ask.
I want to do the best that I can in each and every task.
Thank You for my husband, ever so dear, this I want to say.
For the rest of my life, help me to do the best that I can,
this I pray.

I Awoke With a Start

I awoke with such a start.
I could feel the pounding in my heart.
It was early morn on Christmas Eve
And what a surprise I did receive.
A touch upon my shoulder I did feel.
I could not see anyone, but it was real.
I am sure that my husband sent me a gift.
For my spirits to lift
He wanted me to know
That he still loved me so.
I cried, then upon my face a smile did appear.
I know in my heart that he was still with me here.
A good life together, we did spend
Until his life here on earth did end.
God blessed us, as man and wife, in many ways
And for this I give God glory and praise.
I will love my husband forever and a day.
Someday, again, I will see him, this I pray.

Thinking and Dreaming of the Past

As I sat by the stream flowing ever so fast,
I was thinking and dreaming of the past.
What a wonderful life God has given to me.
There were times of sadness and gladness that were
meant to be.
We don't know how long we have been here on earth.
We know that God has our days numbered from our birth.
So many blessings I have had day by day.
God has been with me all the way.
There were times I felt weak and didn't know what to do.
I prayed to God "Lord, each day help me through."
When I was down and out
Around me, there were friends all about.
I knew and felt that people were praying for me.
When I needed it most, a friend came to my side to be.
Of the past, we cannot dwell, we must go ahead.
Until, in our lifetime, everything God wants of us, is
done and said.
The memories of the past are great.
On bended knee I pray and tell God, of Him, I appreciate.
Sometimes our life seems like a stream that runs downhill.
That is the time that we need to listen to God and be still.
Lord, for in my life, I thank You for each and everything.
Praises to You I will ever sing.

There Are Times We Moan and Complain

Some days, about things, we moan and whine.
When we pray, soon hope and joy will shine.
God wants us to know that, to us, He is always near.
He listens to our cries and prayers with an open ear.
We need to thank the Lord each and every day,
For always being with us in a special way.
Alone and sad, I sometimes feel.
I pray that my attitude, God will heal.
He is always by my side
I know of the right path, for me, He will lead and guide.
Even with prayers, I know there will be days that I
will complain.
But the love of the Lord I will always gain.
Even when there are days that I will still whine.
God's love for me will always shine.
He will always be by my side and never leave me.
He will help me be the best person that I can be.
Thank You Lord, that I can come to You each day.
For all things, I bow my head and pray.

PITY PARTY

A pity party, have you ever had?
You feel like everything around you is going bad.
You're not sure how you are going to get through the day.
Then now is the time to kneel and, to God, pray.
You hear God say, 'child take my hand
And tall I will make you stand'.
Easy, things are not always going to be.
Someday, of why things are happening, you will be
able to see.
Trials and troubles, we all go through.
Remember that God will always be with you.
Through tough times like these we will become strong.
Though it seems like our troubles will be ever so long.
Trust and know that God is with you day by day.
Just let Him lead you all the way.
Don't sit around to pout and whine,
Let the love of God through you shine.
Lord, I want to praise and say thank You
For everything, in my life, that You do.

DAY WAS GLOOMY AND GRAY

Gloomy and gray was the day,
So down on my knees, I knelt to pray.
Sometimes it seems like I am just thinking of me.
In reality, I should focus on the Lord ever to be.
He will guide me and be by my side
If only I will, to Him, listen and abide.
He wants me to have a loving heart and care
And to be able, with another, the love of Jesus to share.
He always knows when I am down and sad.
He wants my day to be happy and glad.
Tears I shed, and times a lot that I cry.
Following Jesus each and every day is what I will try.
He will hold my hand day by day
And sometimes, He will be there to carry me all of the way.
Today, let me be a blessing to someone in need
And to listen to Jesus for Him to lead.
For always being there for me, Lord
I thank You for all of the love, on me, You have poured.

This is a Sad Time

This time for you is very sad indeed.
God wants to comfort you in your time of need.
The memories of your child will always be great.
Someday, when the time is right, he'll meet you at the gate.
God knowns exactly how you feel
And your sorrow and pain, He wants to heal.
Cherish the thoughts and memories of your child
here on earth.
Know that you did the best of everything for him from
his birth.
Your child is now with the heavenly Father above.
God known, for your child, you gave him much love.
At this time of separation from your child, God will
comfort you.
Everyone around you wants to show their care and love too.
Thoughts and prayers are with you day by day.
God will give you peace in a special way.

Trust and Follow the Lord

Direct me in the path of your command, for there will I find
delight. Psalms 119:35
What path is God leading you on? Does it feel right? Don't
allow your emotions to alter your confidence in God.
When He is leading the way, we not only find life, but we
find delight.
Sometimes, it feels like we are going down the wrong
path. I know He will lead me the right way even though it
seems wrong.
We don't like difficult situations in our life, but we all have
them. Call them challenges instead. Difficulties won't
simply go away by calling them by another name.
We all have a choice. Are we going to carry the weight or are
we going to let God carry the load. Trusting God is a pro-
cess. At times, it seems impossible to trust Him when you
are going through a rough time. Be patient when you have
trouble. Pray all the time. Romans 12:12
We need to trust that God is there through all things, and
He will lead us down the right path.
Relying on God has to begin every day. It can be hard to do.
In Psalms 6:3, we cry out "how long Lord, how long."

A BOUQUET OF INSPIRATION

God understands our doubts and fears. We have to trust
that His ways are higher than we can imagine. His timing is
never late.
Lord, help us to trust You completely, that You will lead and
guide us through all things that disturb us and that we will
follow You on the right path.

A Masterpiece Am I

After God made me, He threw away the mold.
There is no other person like me.
But everyone is loved by God, I am told.
Some are fat, thin, short or tall, whoever God created
them to be.
A masterpiece created by God am I
So unique and beautiful in every way.
God knows all of my thoughts and acts until I die,
Hoping that I will follow Him day by day.
God gave me choices for the way that I act.
Things to do, say, and see.
I have only one life to live, that is a fact.
What I decide to do with it is up to me.
For whom I am, God I say thank You.
For all of Your guidance and love.
I ask for forgiveness for my sins I do.
I know that You are watching over me from above.
There is no one like me
Living here on earth.
I am a masterpiece, created by you, ever to be.
I am unique and have been since my birth.
Praise to You oh Lord
For making me special in every way.
And for Your love to me You poured.
I thank You day by day.

A Child of God Am I

I am proud to say, a child of God am I
He provides and cares for me all day and through each nigh.
Sometimes the wrong path I chose to go.
Then I realize that God is there and to me, His love, He
will show.
He wants me to follow, each day, His lead.
I am assured by God that He will take care of my every need.
His love for me is ever so great.
Because of this, each day I can celebrate.
Thank You, God, for, as a child of Yours, You chose me.
Help me to live a good life for all to see.

My Child, I'm Calling You

My child, My child, I am calling you.
Your journey in life is over and through.
Come home to Me, is what I ask.
You have completed your life's every task.
The love you shared with each and every one,
You did this until your life was over and done.
You touched so many a heart.
Day by day you truly did your part.
What a good life you did live
And many blessings to everyone you did give.
At home with the Lord, you now are.
You have touched many lives near and far.
Thank you, My child, for a job well done.
And for this, thanks from each and everyone.

To Your Heavenly Home you Went

You passed from earth to your heavenly home
some time ago.
Each and every day I miss you so.
Sometimes I get angry and mad
And other times, not having you around, I am sad.
I don't know why you had to leave me,
But my love for you will always be.
God had a reason for calling you
He wants me to trust Him through and through.
Some days it seems like all I do is cry.
Then other days, I rejoice, because I know you are with God
ever so high.
You are probably taking care of God's gardens day by day
And other times you spend with the children to play.
It had not been easy for me to take care of everything,
But with God' help, I know praises I can sing.
You were such a wonderful man throughout your life.
Through all things and challenges, we took all things
in strife.
I am so glad of the life, together, we had
I remember and smile thinking of you then no
longer am I sad.

A Special Job

Some years ago, the Lord said to me
'My child, I have a special job for you ever be.
Many children will come your way.
For them, I want you to love and, for them, pray.
Some will have a special need.
I ask that, for them, you will lead.
Your love and care, I want you to share with everyone.
Each day until it is over and done.
Teach them, daily, right from wrong
And help them grow in the Lord ever so strong.
Many lives you will touch
And your love for them will be ever so much.
You will always have an open door.
Your love and kindness, on them, you will pour.
I will give you strength and wisdom if you ask.
For you, I am asking that you do this special task.
My child, day by day, fall on bended knee.
Know that through prayer, you can always come to me.
A job well done to you, I will say someday.
I have been with you through each thing all the way'.
For being with me every day through and through
As Your child, for this task, I say thank You.

There Is a Purpose and a Plan for Me

Lord, I know You have a purpose and a plan for me.
I'm not always sure of what it is to be.
There are times I can't see past the end of my nose.
I feel sorry for myself through all my woes.
Then something happens, and I soon smile.
I know that God is with me along each and every mile.
He reminds me of His love to share.
I'm to let others know that God, for everyone, does
truly care.
I know on God I can rely on and depend.
Somehow, some way His message to me, He will send.
Lead and guide me, Lord, day by day.
Walk beside me in a special way.
Thank You Lord for being so good to me.
Show me daily of the plan for my life ever to be.

Be Thankful

Be thankful for what the Lord asks you to do.
For everything He will see you through.
Sometimes, we don't feel that we can accomplish that task.
Be ready and willing for each task of you, He does ask.
The job may be big or small.
He will lead and guide you, so be ready for His call.
Thank the Lord each and every day for everything.
No matter what, to you, He will bring.
He doesn't ask us to do more than we can do,
Trust in Him, as He is always there for me and you
Prayer and thanks given to the Lord day by day.
Trust Him and He will be by you all the way.
Do each task the best that you can
Show God's love to every woman and man.
Again, I say be ready for His call
The love He has for you, He will never let you fall.
Fall on your knees daily and to Him pray.
In all things, in the Lord, trust and obey.

The Lord Blessed Me With a Special Task

Today, Lord I come to You on bended knee.
I want to praise and thank You for blessing me.
You provided my every need.
Through all things I know, for me, You will lead.
What am I to do today to serve You, I ask.
'You are to love and pray for others,' the Lord says, 'is
your task.'
Lord, I want to trust and obey You in all that I do.
Show me the way daily, through and through.
There are times for a person that I can pray.
I know, for that person, You brought to my mind in a
special way.
When I meet someone, I can greet them with a smile.
I tell them, that for them, I will go the extra mile.
To be able to pray for someone, thank You for choosing me.
I want to encourage them to be the best person that
they can be.
For this special task You have asked me to do.
Lord, again, I say thank You.

Better Days Are Ahead

In life, trials and troubles come about,
Over them we fret, stomp our feet, cry, and shout.
God never promised us a rose garden without nary a thorn.
We need to ask for His leading and guiding each and
every morn.
With His help, we will get through each and every one.
He is with us every day under the sun.
We get frustrated with some things for awhile.
Then we sit down and rest and soon, upon our faces,
comes a smile.
To handle all the problems that come our way
Go to God and kneel and pray.
God bless you in all that you do
Remember, through tough times, God will carry
you through.
Now I will pray for you, my friend.
Good wishes for better days ahead, to you I send.

Praises and Songs In My Heart

For God, praises and songs I have in my heart
And ask Him daily to help me do my part.
He walks quietly by my side.
He tells me, in Him, I should abide.
He tries to show me how to go the right way
He does this for me each and every day.
For me, right choices He wants me to make
And of His love, He wants me to take.
With everyone, He wants me to share
That for each person, He truly does care.
Sometimes we think we can do things on our own.
God want us to know that, with Him, we are never alone.
For His help and guidance, on Him we should call.
We hope that by doing this, we don't stumble and fall.
I know that my prayers and praises, You, God listen
to and hear.
Thank You God for always being ever so near.

White Staircase Shining in the Light

I had a dream one night.
I saw a white staircase shining in the light.
Very curious was I
To see if the staircase reached the sky.
I started to climb each stair
Taking each step with care.
Suddenly, I heard a voice say
'My child, I am not ready for you today.
Go back down and finish each task
Of all the things, of you, I ask
When I am ready for you, your name I will call.
Then you can climb up the staircase walking tall.
Trust in me in all that you do.
I will be by your side through and through.
Be proud of who you are in all you do and say.
Show everyone around you how to live the right way.
Now is not the time to climb the staircase.
For you yet, there are many more days of praise.
Child, you are very special to Me.
And someday you will with Me ever be.'

I May Not Be Able, But I Am Willing

At times, I think I'm not able to do what the Lord does ask.
Yet I tell Him I am willing to do the task.
He will give me grace to be able to do what I am to do.
He will strengthen me in all the days through.
He chose me to be a willing servant all of the time
And obeying Him is never a crime.
On the Lord I can always lean, this I know.
His love for me, in many ways, He does show.
Sometimes I just have to change my attitude.
Praying and honoring Him is how I can show my gratitude.
For the things I am to do, thank You, Lord for choosing me.
I pray that the people around me, of Your love they will see.
Lord, You are a loving and gracious God to one and all.
Give each of us the strength to walk ever so tall.
Let me do the tasks You ask of me in stride.
I am willing to do these things with love and pride.

Why, God, Why

Why, God, Why
Must there be tragedies and people die?
Why, God, why
Must there be pain and people cry?
Why, God, why
Can't people be friends by and by?
Why do people hate their fellow man
And everything on this land?
The answer is not ours to know
For our lives, it must be onward we go.
Sometimes it seems as though life is hard to bear.
But, for us, Jesus Christ will be there.
Those who trust in the Lord can endure all
Even when there are days that downward we fall.
Get down on your knees to pray.
Thank God for all things day by day.
For the answer to these questions is to trust in the Lord.
Praise Him for unto us, the love He has poured.
Why, God, why is what we all want to know.
We ask for Your guidance of which way to go.
Lord, be with us each and every day
For Your love, comfort, and protection, we pray.

WHAT IF MARY DID BELIEVE

What if Mary, Mother of Jesus, in abortion did believe?
Then of Jesus Christ's mercy, we would never receive.
The world would have been a much different place
And we would never get to meet God face to face.
Abortion, in a minute, will stop a heartbeat
And of that baby, the world would never meet.
People say, 'the whales we must save'
But it is okay to send an unborn baby to the grave?
Sometimes we forget where our priorities are
And for the rest of our lives, we must bear the scar.
Because God saw that Jesus was born of Mary,
His love for us will never vary.
Remember that babies, to us, are God's gift.
For this, thanks and praises, to God, we should lift.

I Am a Mother

A mother, God has created me to be,
To share love and caring to all that I see.
Being a mother is not an easy task.
Sometimes, it is hard to please children for all that they ask.
When they fall and scrape their knee
They come running and want hugs and kisses from me.
There are times that I can only hold them very tight
And pray for them each day and every night.
I am not a perfect mom, this I know.
Each child that comes my way, my love to them I can show.
Without God by my side, I could not make it through the day.
He leads, guides, and loves me in His special way.
There are days of being a mother, I will stumble and fall,
But I am there for every child, big or small.
Being a mother, I will, for all my children, do the best that I can.
I know for me, God, this is Your plan.
Help me every day for Your leading, this I pray.
Lord, for trusting me to be a mother, thanks and praises I give to
You each day.

Dandelions Everywhere

Of a dandelion, what do you think?
They seem to appear in just a blink.
Their seeds scatter, and into the wind they blow
And land where another dandelion will grow.
Their roots grow ever so deep,
But in reality, they are not something we want to keep
Maybe like them, we should try to be,
To have our roots deep in Jesus Christ for all to see.
As the seeds blow in the wind and scatter
Maybe one person will come to know that Jesus Christ
does matter.
We need to spread the word to each and everyone
Until our life here on earth is over and done.
We never know where each seed will land,
But we know spreading that seed is what God has planned.
The next time, of a dandelion you see,
Think about how their seeds float ever so free.
Some people may think of you as a bother, as a weed.
God planned that you are to spread the word by
planting a seed.
Your seed will land and, with nurturing, will grow.
Remember the seeds that you plant are so people, of God,
will know.
Scatter your seeds and plant them ever so deep.
The truth of God is for all to know and keep.

Forgive and Pray

When someone has done something to you in a wrong way
For that person, forgive and pray.
The more that you forgive and pray, the more blessings will
be given to you.
Be faithful and do what the Lord asks you to do.
You may never see the result of that one.
God knows what needs to be done.
Prayer does not change God, but prayer will change you.
Pray continuously the whole day through.
Sometimes, for that person, it is hard to forgive.
By doing this, blessings will be given to you as long as you
shall live.
Thank God for the trials that He gives to you every day.
He will do what is best for you in a special way.
God is in control of everything.
Through these times, His love to you, He will bring
Help me forgive and be faithful until, for me, God does call.
Let me be an example to one and all.
To You, God, I lift my hands in praise.
I need to ask forgiveness of my sins all of my days
Help me to show my love and forgiveness to those who have
hurt me in a
certain way.
Thank You for Your love and blessings you give to me
day by day.

A Bouquet of Inspiration

May the God of hope fill you with all the Joy and peace as you trust in Him, so that you may overflow with hope by the power of the Holy Spirit.
Romans 15:13
Oh Lord, you will obtain peace for us, for you have indeed done for us all your words. Isaiah 26:12
Now may the Lord of Peace, Himself, always give you peace in every way. The Lord be with you all. 2 Thessalonians 3:16
Without God, there can be no hope.

Printed in the USA
CPSIA information can be obtained
at www.ICGtesting.com
CBHW071931090924
14162CB00008B/187